Could Would You?

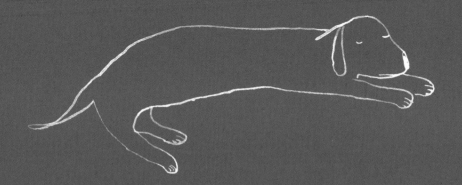

ACKNOWLEDGEMENTS

Thank you, Rosalind Price and Sue Flockhart, for being lovely to work with. Thank you, Andrew, Sandra and Mary for helping. Thank you like an autumn moon to MZ, Jiri and Nan, and Monnie Sue, who keep me going in books.

Kane/Miller Book Publishers, Inc.
First American Edition 2007
by Kane/Miller Book Publishers, Inc.
La Jolla, California

Kane/Miller Book Publishers, Inc.
P.O. Box 8515
La Jolla, CA 92038
www.kanemiller.com

Library of Congress Control Number: 2007921048
Printed and bound in China
1 2 3 4 5 6 7 8 9 10

ISBN: 978-1-933605-45-6

Could You?
Would You?

Trudy White

Kane/Miller
BOOK PUBLISHERS

Contents

For Louis

Could you fall asleep
with all these animals?

Would you wake up early
or sleep in late?

What is the best thing about you?

I saved someone from drowning.

I can count backwards
from 1,000,000 in threes.

I can flip pancakes.

I can see ghosts.

Snails like me.

I can swing higher than anyone.

I notice things that other people don't.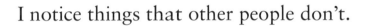

I can tell a Stegosaurus from a Diprotodon.

my laugh

Draw a picture of yourself

How many teeth do you have?

Have you lost any?

How wide can you stretch your arms out?

Would you like
hair like this?

How tall
are you in
centimeters?

In bananas?

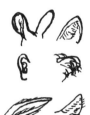

What shape are your ears?

Do you have a soft
mouse voice or a gruff
bear voice?

How would someone find you in a crowd?

Could you run an all-night race?

Would you stop for naps
or would you sleep later?

9

Can you wiggle your ears
like a rabbit?

Can you peel an orange
in one long snake?

What is the longest daisy chain
you have ever made?

Can you walk without
making a sound?

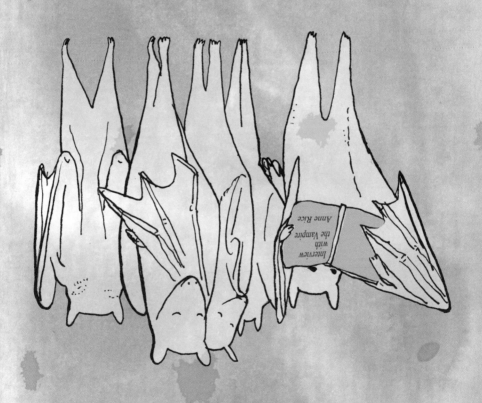

Can you read upside-down?

Would you like to be able to:

stand on one leg?

skate along a railing?

somersault?

dive off the top board?

walk on land

ski backwards?

leap in the air?

run up walls?

curl your tongue?

How would you learn to do these things?

Could you recognize your family
with your eyes shut?

Would you know their voices,
their smell, or something else?

Draw a picture of your family

How many people
are there
in your family?

Where did the
people in your
family grow up?

What do you
like doing
with your family?

17

How did your mom
get to school
when she was a girl?

What did your dad do
when he was a boy?

How is your day different
from your grandma's
when she was little?

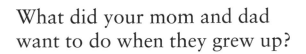

What did your mom and dad
want to do when they grew up?

19

Could you live here?

up high

in a city

in a modern house

by a river

in a pocket

in a tree

by the sea

on ice

in the desert

in a teapot

in a house your
parents built

on wheels

by a busy road

in a house with
a big garden

Or would you rather
live here?

What is the best thing about where you live?

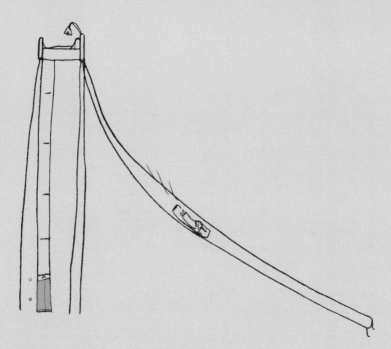

If your house had a secret room,
what would be in there?

What is the loudest spot
in your house?

Where do you like to sit?

What can you
hear when you
close your eyes?

waves crashing

dogs barking

someone playing
a saxophone

Draw a map of the rooms in your house

Put in:

the fastest way
to go outside
from your
room

elevators or stairs

the warmest place

the smelliest place

the most interesting
thing about your house

the hole
into
the roof

any big spiders
that live there

cat or dog
doors

the best place
to hide

Where do you like to walk from your house?

What things do you notice?

my house

two loud dogs live here

figs falling off a tree

cat lane

a house being built

school

We walk to the park every day.

Could you do the same thing all day?
Would you:

build?

carry?

listen?

cook?

talk?

look at clouds?

feed animals?

comb?

sort?

dig?

explore?

draw?

dress up?

What would you like to do when you are bigger?

look after animals

fight fires

travel the world

style hair

write books

plant trees

own 50 cats

sail a boat

run a shop

Would you like to be famous for doing something?

31

How will you change as you grow up?

What will you do when you are very old?

What stories will you tell
children who visit you?

What special thing will you
keep until you are old?

What will you
give away?

Where will people live in the future?

How will people travel?

What would you create to make
your house more comfortable?

How could
you make
school
better?

How will people
communicate?

Could you keep up
with a cheetah?

Would you like to
dance with animals
or look at plants?

What animal would you like as a pet?

What would you name it?

Flopsy

Coco   Buttons

Where would it sleep?

What would it do while you were out?

What sort of animal would you like to be?

Would you be friends with people?

Or not?

Would you like to:

sniff like a dog?

dig like a wombat?

nibble like a rabbit?

reach like a giraffe?

Would you swap your arms for wings?

You could see things from the air.

You could go wherever you liked.

maybe not

41

Do you have a favorite plant?

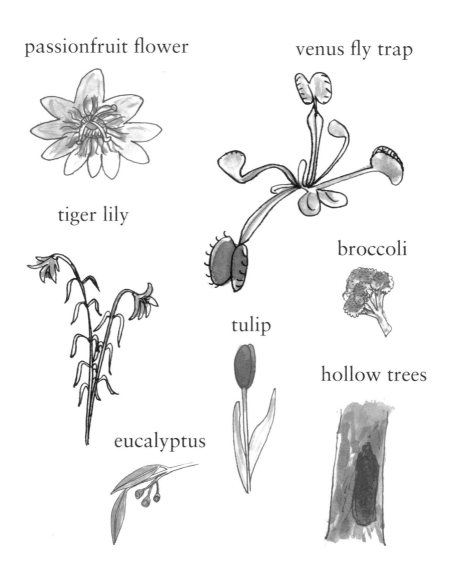

passionfruit flower

venus fly trap

tiger lily

broccoli

tulip

hollow trees

eucalyptus

Draw a picture of the most dangerous
flower in the world.

It might have:

sharp thorns

prickles

stinky sap

slimy traps

poisonous berries

What happens if you go too close?

Could you learn every language
in the world?

Would you learn each new one faster
or would you muddle them up?

Make a list of words
you like saying

ace

wonder

moon

wobble

dog

peach

What words are you
not allowed to say?

What do you say instead?

What is the longest word you know?

archaeopteryx

What would you do if
everyone spoke a language
you couldn't understand?

What would you say
if you could talk to
animals?

How many different ways could you send a message?

pigeon

email

mail

singing telegram

phone

walkie talkie

skywriting

Will you marry me Tina?

billboard

rocks
on the
footpath

How do animals talk?

ear wiggling   tail wagging   teeth baring

Could you cheer someone up
if they were feeling sad?

Would you talk
or go for a walk?

What makes you smile?

big goldfish in a pond
pineapple
my cat drinking milk

When do you feel content?

hugging my dad
eating dessert
playing with my toys

What makes you grumpy?

going to the bank
being in the car
waiting for dinner

What makes you miserable?

my mom is sick
my friend is moving away
I'm left out of the game

What makes you angry?

it wasn't my fault
Mom says no!
I have to eat it all

When do you feel loved?

Grandpa and I play all day
a letter from my auntie
a special present

What is the funniest thing you can remember?

What is the scariest thing
you have ever lived through?

Do you ever feel
bigger than usual?   Or smaller?

What helps you feel better
if you're sad?

Could you imagine
waking up one morning
as a baby again?

Would you try to tell someone
or not?

Do you remember being a baby?

Who did you like to be with?

What was the first word you said?

Do you still have your favorite toy?

What did you like to wear
when you were little?

What did you collect?

model horses

shells

blocks

train tickets

airplanes

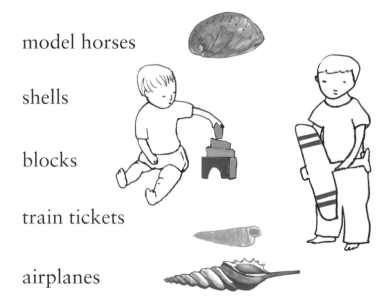

Did you have imaginary friends?

What was the first painting you did?

What was your
favorite story?

What did you think
thunder was?

Did you ever
run away?

Were you noisy or quiet?

Could you survive without food for a week?

Would you eat a meal
that a cat had cooked?

What is the best meal you have ever eaten?

What would you cook for a feast?

How many different fruits and
vegetables have you tried?

   yellow
pepper

dates

   lychees

bok choy

   starfruit

avocado

   kiwi fruit

broad beans

   passionfruit

Is there a food you can't stand?

What would you
like to do with it?

Could you bathe in a hot spring
in the snow?

Would you jump in quickly
or slide in slowly?

Would you like to:

bathe in a laundry sink?

wash in a river?

share a sparrow's dust bath?

soap up with an octopus?

soak in a public bath house?

brush your hair on an airplane?

clean your teeth on a bus?

rinse under a waterfall?

lie in a puddle?

Could you travel to outer space?

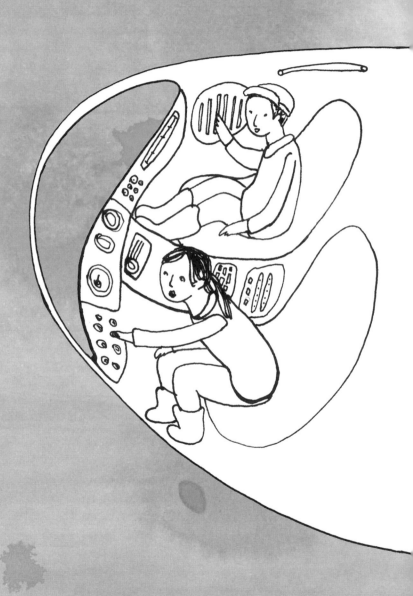

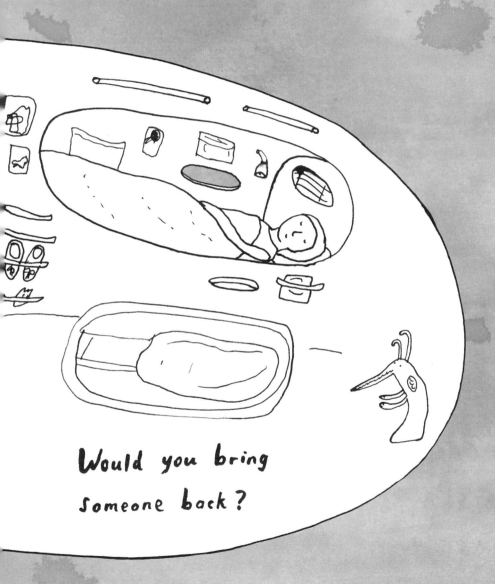

Would you bring
someone back?

What is the fastest thing you have ever traveled in?

How would you like to travel around?

walking

on stilts

on an elephant

through a tunnel

on a toboggan

in a submarine

in a speedboat

on a scooter

on a monorail

in a flying bed

If you could swim underwater,
where would you go?

What would you like to see and do?

swing on a rope over
the Danube River

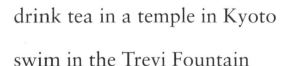

eat an ice cream
under the Eiffel Tower

drink tea in a temple in Kyoto

swim in the Trevi Fountain

cook noodles
in Beijing

ski in the
Swiss Alps

sleep in a hammock
in Vanuatu

talk to a parrot
in Brazil

make a
sandcastle at
Bondi beach

Could you help someone
who was having a baby?

Would you bring them
a cup of tea?

Would you help
tidy the house?

Where were you before you were born?

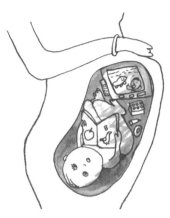

What time were you born?

Did you take a long time to come out?

Would you like a new baby in your family?

Have you ever
seen a baby or
an animal being
born?

Do you know someone who has died?

What do you remember about them?

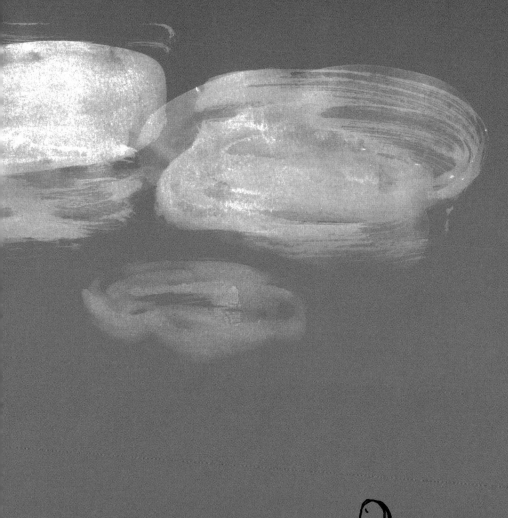

Where did they go?

Could you live in a place where the weather never changes?

ETROIT, MICHIGAN

Would you miss anything?

How do you know when it's Spring?

It rains for days.
The grass is suddenly long.
Flowers bloom≈cdjh x.

How do you know when it's Summer?

Even my mom eats popsicles.
I wear a bathing suit all day.
We go to the beach after dinner.

How do you know when it's autumn?

Our pumpkins are ready.
Leaves go brown.
I notice the wind blowing.

How do you know when it's winter?

We collect firewood.
We have to scrape ice
    off the car windows.

I am allowed to sleep inside the house.

Does it ever snow in your street?

How close have you
been to lightning?

What is the biggest
hailstone you have seen?

How do you cool down
when your house is too hot?

Can you see stars from your bedroom?

Could you answer these questions another day?

Would your answers be the same
or would they change?

Trudy White
likes to draw pictures and write
and ask lots of questions.

What animal would you like
as a pet?

Actually, I would like a few different animals:

a miniature lemur that could swing around the branches
of a potted plant in my studio,

a polar bear to cuddle when I am cold,

a team of sled dogs to help me think,

and a barn owl that would sharpen pencils with its beak
(not just mangle them),

but only if they make friends with Gogo,
who cooks the best snacks a cat ever made.